ANATOMY OF AN EMPLOYMENT SCAM

Defeat Common Scams With Common Sense

Hon. Thomas Mitchell, DD, PhD

Produced at: TomCatt Studios, Stockton, California, USA

A

Copyright

© 2024

Hon. Thomas Mitchell, DD, PhD

All rights reserved

The characters and events portrayed in this book are fictitious. Any similarity to real persons, living or dead, is coincidental and not intended by the author.

No part of this book may be reproduced, or stored in a retrieval system, or transmitted in any form or by any means, electronic, mechanical, photocopying, recording, or otherwise, without express written permission of the publisher.

Cover design by: Author

B

Table of Contents

Copyright .... A

Chapter 1: Introduction to the Employment Scam 1

Chapter 2: Understanding How the Employment Scam Works 4

Chapter 3: Psychological Tactics and Why the Employment Scam Succeeds 7

Chapter 4: Similarities Between the Employment Scam and Other Common Scams 12

Chapter 5: Red Flags to Watch Out for in the Employment Scam 15

Chapter 6: Recognizing the Signs of the Employment Scam 19

Chapter 7: Taking Action When Confronted with the Employment Scam 23

Chapter 8: Reporting the Employment Scam and Seeking Legal Help 27

Chapter 9: Recovering from the Financial and Emotional Impact of the Employment Scam 30

Chapter 10: Supporting a Friend Who is Falling for the Employment Scam 33

Chapter 11: Conclusion.. 38

Chapter 12: A Message of Hope: 41

Chapter 13: Additional Resources for Protection Against Employment Scams 44

C

Chapter 14: Author's Closing Thoughts and Acknowledgments..........47

D

E

Chapter 1: Introduction to the Employment Scam

Understanding the Scope and Impact of the Problem

1.1 Defining the Employment Scam and Its Prevalence in Society

In today's digital age, the internet has revolutionized the way we search for jobs and connect with potential employers. However, along with these advancements, a dark underbelly has emerged – the employment scam. The employment scam refers to fraudulent schemes designed to deceive individuals seeking employment opportunities. These scams have infiltrated various platforms, including online job boards, social media, and email exchanges, preying on vulnerable job seekers who are eager to secure employment.

According to recent reports, the prevalence of employment scams has been skyrocketing, with millions of people falling victim each year. These scammers operate globally, targeting individuals from all walks of life and across industries. It is essential to understand the extent of this problem to effectively combat it and protect potential victims from harm.

1.2 Examining the Consequences of Falling Victim to the Employment Scam

Falling victim to an employment scam can have severe consequences that extend far beyond financial loss. Victims may experience feelings of embarrassment, shame, and betrayal as their trust is exploited by scammers posing as legitimate employers. Moreover, victims often suffer significant financial setbacks due to stolen personal information, fraudulent charges, or even drained bank accounts.

Additionally, victims can face long-term emotional and psychological effects from the trauma of being deceived. These consequences may include anxiety, depression, loss of self-esteem, and a general sense of mistrust towards future job opportunities or online interactions. Understanding the full range of consequences empowers individuals to recognize the importance of prevention and take proactive measures against falling victim to an employment scam.

1.3 Highlighting Real-Life Stories of Individuals Who Have Been Affected by the Scam

To provide readers with a firsthand understanding of the impact of employment scams, this chapter will present real-life stories from individuals who have fallen prey to these schemes. These stories will encompass different demographics, professions, and outcomes. By sharing these personal experiences, readers can empathize with victims and gain insight into the deceptive tactics employed by scammers.

These stories will serve as cautionary tales and motivate readers to take preventive measures when searching for employment opportunities online. Furthermore, they will act as a reminder that anyone can become a target of employment scams.

1.4 Outlining the Purpose and Structure of the Book

The purpose of this book is to equip readers with knowledge and strategies to protect themselves from employment scams. By understanding how these scams operate, recognizing warning signs, and taking appropriate action, individuals can significantly reduce their vulnerability to these fraudulent schemes.

The book will guide readers through various aspects of the employment scam, including its prevalence, tactics used by scammers, psychological manipulation techniques employed, similarities with other common scams, red flags to watch out for, and steps to take when confronted with a scam. Additionally, it will provide resources for reporting scams, seeking legal help, recovering from financial and emotional impacts, supporting friends who may be falling victim to scams, and rebuilding after a scam incident.

1.5 Setting the Tone for Empowering Readers Against Scammers

This book aims to provide a comprehensive understanding of the employment scam while maintaining an empowering tone throughout. By arming readers with knowledge and practical tools to stay vigilant and informed, they will be better equipped to navigate their job search journeys safely.

While scams continue to evolve in complexity and sophistication, awareness and education remain powerful weapons against scammers' malicious intentions. Together with collective efforts within communities and law enforcement agencies, individuals can reclaim their power in combating this pervasive problem. Let us embark on this journey together - unraveling the anatomy of the employment scam - so that we can empower ourselves and build a safer online environment for all.

Chapter 2: Understanding How the Employment Scam Works

Unraveling the Tactics Employed by Scammers

2.1 Explaining the Step-by-Step Process Scammers Use to Deceive Victims

To effectively protect oneself from employment scams, it is crucial to understand the step-by-step process scammers employ. This chapter will delve into the intricacies of how scammers operate, providing readers with a comprehensive understanding of the tactics employed.

By breaking down the scam process, readers will gain insight into how scammers manipulate job seekers and exploit their vulnerability. From creating enticing job postings to establishing false credibility, scammers follow a carefully constructed plan to deceive their victims. Through a detailed examination of each stage, readers will uncover the sophisticated techniques employed by scammers and be better prepared to identify and avoid falling victim to these deceptive tactics.

2.2 Analyzing the Psychology Behind Manipulation and Exploitation in Employment Scams

Understanding the psychology behind manipulation and exploitation is key to comprehending why employment scams are successful. In this section, we will explore the psychological factors at play during different stages of the scam, providing readers with an in-depth analysis of how scammers exploit human emotions and cognitive biases.

By employing persuasion techniques, scammers carefully craft narratives that appeal to individuals' desires for financial security, meaningful work, and career advancement. They exploit psychological vulnerabilities such as trust, fear, urgency, and confirmation bias to establish control over their victims. Exploring these psychological tactics equips readers with the knowledge needed to recognize manipulative strategies and protect themselves against deception.

2.3 Investigating Common Platforms Where Employment Scams Thrive

Employment scams have found fertile ground within specific platforms where job seekers congregate. This section will examine common platforms such as online job boards, social media platforms, and email exchanges that scammers exploit to target potential victims.

By understanding the characteristics of these platforms and the inherent risks associated with them, readers can make informed decisions about where and how they search for job opportunities online. Familiarity with the common tactics used on different platforms will enable readers to adopt a cautious approach when interacting with potential employers in these spaces.

2.4 Discussing the Role of Social Media and Technology in Facilitating These Scams

The advent of social media and technological advancements has provided scammers with new avenues and tools to carry out employment scams effectively. In this section, we will explore how scammers leverage social media platforms and technology to their advantage.

From creating fake profiles on LinkedIn to exploiting messaging apps or video interviews, scammers adapt quickly to evolving technology trends. By examining these tactics and discussing real-life examples, readers will gain an understanding of the role that social media and technology play in facilitating employment scams. Armed with this knowledge, they can navigate online interactions more effectively and identify potential red flags.

2.5 Providing Examples and Case Studies to Illustrate Key Concepts

To enhance readers' comprehension of the tactics discussed throughout this chapter, relevant examples and case studies will be provided. These real-world scenarios will highlight how scammers implement various strategies during different stages of the scam process.

By presenting concrete examples, readers will be able to contextualize the theoretical concepts discussed earlier in the chapter. These case studies will underscore the importance of vigilance and critical thinking when engaging in job search activities online.

By unraveling the tactics employed by scammers, readers will develop a deeper understanding of how employment scams operate. Armed with this knowledge, they will be better equipped to identify warning signs early on and protect themselves from falling victim to these fraudulent schemes.

Chapter 3: Psychological Tactics and Why the Employment Scam Succeeds

Unveiling the Psychological Tricks Scammers Employ

3.1 Examining the Psychological Vulnerabilities That Scammers Exploit

In order to understand how employment scammers succeed in deceiving their victims, it is crucial to delve into the psychological vulnerabilities that scammers exploit. These vulnerabilities can vary from individual to individual, but scammers are skilled at identifying and exploiting common weaknesses.

Some of the psychological vulnerabilities that scammers target include:

- Desperation and financial vulnerability: Many individuals who fall prey to employment scams are facing financial difficulties or are desperate to find a job. Scammers exploit this vulnerability by offering enticing job opportunities that promise high salaries or quick financial relief.

- Trust and belief in authority: Scammers often impersonate reputable organizations or use official-sounding terms to gain the trust of their victims. By presenting themselves as authoritative figures, scammers manipulate victims into believing they are legitimate employers.

- Hope and optimism: Job seekers are naturally hopeful and optimistic about finding employment. Scammers take advantage of this positive mindset by offering unrealistic promises and appealing job opportunities that seem too good to be true.

- Fear and urgency: Scammers frequently use fear tactics, such as creating a sense of urgency or emphasizing limited time offers, to pressure victims into making hasty decisions. This manipulative technique preys on individuals' anxiety about missing out on potential job opportunities.

3.2 Discussing Persuasion Techniques Used by Scammers to Gain Trust and Credibility

Scammers employ various persuasion techniques to establish trust and credibility with their victims. These techniques are designed to make victims more susceptible to manipulation and less likely to question the legitimacy of the scam.

Some common persuasion techniques used by employment scammers include:

- Social proof: Scammers may create fake testimonials or positive reviews to give the illusion of credibility. By presenting themselves as having successfully helped others secure jobs, scammers aim to gain the trust of their victims.

- Authority positioning: Scammers often present themselves as industry experts, using jargon and professional language to establish credibility. They may claim affiliation with well-known companies or institutions, further enhancing their perceived authority.

- Reciprocity: Scammers may offer small favors or assistance initially, creating a sense of indebtedness in their victims. This reciprocity tactic makes victims more likely to comply with subsequent requests or provide personal information.

- Emotional manipulation: Scammers may appeal to victims' emotions, using sympathy or compassion to gain their trust. By exploiting victims' vulnerabilities, scammers increase the likelihood of successful manipulation.

3.3 Investigating the Role of Fear and Urgency in Manipulating Victims

Fear and urgency are powerful psychological triggers that scammers exploit to manipulate their victims. By creating a sense of urgency, scammers increase the pressure on victims and reduce their likelihood of critically evaluating the situation.

Some ways in which scammers use fear and urgency in employment scams include:

- Limited time offers: Scammers often claim that job opportunities are available for a limited time only, pressuring victims into making quick decisions without thoroughly researching or verifying the legitimacy of the opportunity.

- Threats of missed opportunities: Scammers may imply that failing to seize an opportunity immediately will result in missed chances for career advancement or financial gain. This fear of missing out pushes victims into taking action without proper consideration.

- Impersonation of authority figures: Scammers may pose as high-ranking executives or government officials, leveraging their supposed authority to induce fear in victims. The fear of potential consequences drives victims to comply with the scammers' demands.

- False sense of urgency: Scammers create a false sense of urgency by claiming there is intense competition for a particular job position or that multiple candidates are being considered. This urgency can lead victims to overlook warning signs or red flags in their eagerness to secure the job.

3.4 Exploring Cognitive Biases and How They Contribute to Falling for Scams

Cognitive biases play a significant role in why individuals fall for scams, including employment scams. These biases are inherent shortcuts in our thinking processes that can cloud judgment and lead individuals to make irrational decisions.

Some cognitive biases relevant to falling for employment scams include:

- Anchoring bias: Victims may fixate on specific details presented by scammers, such as high salary figures or prestigious job titles, without critically evaluating the overall legitimacy of the opportunity.

- Confirmation bias: Once individuals have become emotionally invested in a particular job opportunity, they tend to seek information that confirms their initial positive impression. This bias can prevent them from recognizing warning signs or contradictory evidence.

- Availability bias: Victims may rely heavily on easily retrievable information, such as positive testimonials provided by scammers, while disregarding contradictory information. This bias can distort their perception of the legitimacy of the opportunity.

- Trust bias: People tend to default to trusting others unless given a reason not to. Scammers exploit this bias by imitating trustworthy individuals or organizations, manipulating victims into assuming they are dealing with genuine employers.

3.5 Offering Strategies for Strengthening Mental Resilience Against Psychological Tactics

To protect oneself from falling victim to employment scams, it is essential to develop mental resilience against the psychological tactics employed by scammers. By being aware of these tactics and building critical thinking skills, individuals can better evaluate job opportunities and identify potential scams.

Some strategies for strengthening mental resilience against psychological tactics include:

- Develop skepticism: Cultivate a healthy level of skepticism when evaluating job offers or interacting with potential employers. Question claims that seem too good to be true and conduct thorough research before proceeding further.

- Verify information independently: Instead of relying solely on information provided by scammers, seek independent verification through official company websites, contact numbers, or industry associations. Avoid using contact information provided by the potentially fraudulent party.

- Take time before making decisions: Don't succumb to pressure or urgency imposed by scammers. Take ample time to evaluate offers, consult trusted advisors, and gather all necessary information before committing to any decision.

- Be vigilant for red flags: Familiarize yourself with common red flags associated with employment scams, such as requests for personal information upfront, payment requests from potential employers, or unprofessional communication methods. Recognizing these warning signs can help you avoid potential scams.

By understanding how scammers employ psychological tactics and implementing strategies for stronger mental resilience, individuals can significantly reduce their vulnerability to employment scams. The next chapter will explore similarities between the employment scam and other common scams, providing insights into shared patterns and techniques used by scammers across different fraudulent schemes.

Chapter 4: Similarities Between the Employment Scam and Other Common Scams

Identifying Shared Patterns and Techniques

4.1 Examining Common Elements Across Various Types of Scams, such as Phishing and Pyramid Schemes

While the employment scam may seem unique in its targeting of job seekers, it shares many similarities with other common scams. This chapter will explore the common elements that exist across various types of scams, such as phishing scams and pyramid schemes.

By analyzing these shared patterns and techniques, readers can gain a deeper understanding of the tactics employed by scammers in different contexts. This knowledge will not only help individuals recognize potential scams but also allow them to draw parallels and apply lessons learned from other forms of fraud to protect themselves against employment scams.

4.2 Drawing Parallels Between Employment Scams and Romance Scams or Investment Fraud

One significant overlap between employment scams and other common scams is the use of manipulation and deception to exploit victims' trust. For example, romance scams involve perpetrators establishing fake relationships online to gain victims' affections and then requesting money under false pretenses. Similarly, investment fraud schemes rely on promises of high returns to lure unsuspecting individuals into investing their hard-earned money.

By examining the similarities between these scams and the employment scam, readers can become aware of the tactics scammers commonly employ and enhance their ability to detect and avoid falling victim to deceptive schemes.

4.3 Analyzing Common Characteristics of Scammers Regardless of Scam Type

Scammers often exhibit recurring traits regardless of the specific scam they are running. This section will delve into the common characteristics that scammers possess, such as manipulative behavior, persuasive communication skills, and a knack for exploiting vulnerabilities.

Understanding these commonalities can help individuals develop a comprehensive profile of scammers, making it easier to identify potential fraudsters before falling prey to their schemes. By recognizing warning signs and red flags, readers can protect themselves by avoiding engaging with scammers altogether.

4.4 Highlighting Lessons Learned from Other Scams to Prevent Falling for an Employment Scam

Drawing upon the lessons learned from various types of scams, readers will discover valuable insights that can be applied specifically to avoid falling for an employment scam. By adopting a multi-faceted approach to scam prevention, individuals can strengthen their overall scam awareness and build effective defenses against manipulative tactics.

This section will provide actionable strategies derived from the experiences of victims who have fallen for different scams and experts in the field of scam prevention. These strategies may include tips on conducting thorough research, verifying legitimacy, recognizing warning signs, and seeking advice from trusted sources.

4.5 Discussing Legal Actions Taken Against Scam Networks and Their Impact on Prevention Efforts

Efforts to combat scams extend beyond individual prevention measures. This section will explore legal actions taken against scam networks and the potential impact they have on preventing future scams.

By highlighting successful legal actions and their consequences for scammers, individuals will better understand the significance of reporting scams and cooperating with law enforcement agencies. Additionally, readers will gain insight into how collective efforts from authorities and individuals can disrupt scam operations and contribute to a safer online environment.

Understanding the similarities between employment scams and other common scams is crucial in equipping individuals with a holistic understanding of scam tactics. By identifying shared patterns and techniques, readers can enhance their scam detection skills, empowering them to avoid falling victim to various fraudulent schemes, including employment scams.

Chapter 5: Red Flags to Watch Out for in the Employment Scam

Spotting Warning Signs Early On

5.1 Providing a Comprehensive List of Red Flags Specific to Employment Scams, Including Unrealistic Promises and Suspicious Job Postings

Recognizing red flags is crucial in protecting oneself from falling victim to an employment scam. In this chapter, we will provide readers with a comprehensive list of warning signs specific to employment scams. These include unrealistic promises or guarantees, such as high salaries for minimal work, no experience required, or immediate job offers without an interview process.

Additionally, suspicious job postings can serve as red flags. These may include job descriptions that lack specific details about the company or position, vague requirements or qualifications, or misspellings and grammatical errors. Furthermore, unusual email addresses or contact information associated with the job posting can indicate the presence of scammers.

By familiarizing themselves with these red flags, readers will be able to identify potentially fraudulent job opportunities and take appropriate action to protect themselves.

5.2 Detailing Common Tactics Scammers Use During Interviews and Job Offer Stages

Scammers often employ various tactics during interviews and job offer stages to manipulate their victims further. In this section, we will delve into these tactics, providing readers with insights on what to watch out for and how to respond.

For instance, scammers may conduct interviews via instant messaging platforms or phone calls instead of in-person or video interviews. They may ask unusual or invasive questions that legitimate employers would not typically ask, such as financial information or personal identification details. Scammers may also pressure victims into hasty decisions by creating a sense of urgency or emphasizing limited availability of the job opportunity.

By understanding these common tactics, readers will be better prepared to navigate these interactions and recognize when they are being targeted by scammers.

5.3 Discussing Discrepancies Between Legitimate Job Opportunities and Employment Scams

To further equip readers with the skills to distinguish between legitimate job opportunities and scams, this section will highlight discrepancies commonly present in employment scams.

These discrepancies can manifest in various ways. For example, scammers may claim affiliation with reputable companies or organizations without any substantial evidence or legitimacy. They may request payment upfront for supposed training materials or equipment, whereas legitimate employers usually cover these expenses themselves. Additionally, scammers may request personal information that is unnecessary for a typical job application process, such as passport details or social security numbers.

Understanding these disparities will enable readers to critically evaluate job offers and identify potential scams before becoming entangled in them.

5.4 Outlining Ways to Verify the Legitimacy of Potential Employers or Recruiters

Verifying the legitimacy of potential employers or recruiters is a crucial aspect of protecting oneself from employment scams. This section will outline effective methods for conducting thorough research and due diligence.

Readers will learn techniques such as searching for the company's official website and scrutinizing its content for inconsistencies or generic information. They will also be encouraged to reach out directly to the company's official contact information found through reliable sources rather than solely relying on communication channels provided by recruiters.

Additionally, readers will explore strategies for checking the company's reputation through online reviews and professional networking platforms. By utilizing these methods, individuals can verify whether the job opportunity is genuine or a potential employment scam.

5.5 Sharing Real-Life Examples to Help Readers Recognize Warning Signs in Different Scenarios

To enhance readers' understanding of red flags, this section will provide real-life examples that illustrate common warning signs encountered in different scenarios.

These examples will encompass a range of employment scam tactics, including fictitious companies requesting personal information upfront, promises of unrealistic pay rates for minimal work, and manipulative interview processes designed to create a false sense of urgency.

By examining these real-life scenarios, readers will become more adept at recognizing similar warning signs if they encounter them in their own job search journeys.

Armed with knowledge about the specific red flags associated with employment scams, readers will become increasingly skilled at identifying potential scams early on in order to protect themselves from falling victim.

Prevention is key in combating the employment scam epidemic, and by staying vigilant and informed, individuals can mitigate their risk and contribute to a safer online environment for all.

Chapter 6: Recognizing the Signs of the Employment Scam

Empowering Readers to Trust Their Instincts

6.1 Encouraging readers to listen to their intuition when something feels off in a job application process

In the world of employment scams, it is crucial for individuals to trust their instincts. Often, our intuition can provide valuable insights and serve as an early warning system when something feels off during the job application process. These gut feelings should not be ignored but rather explored further to ensure one's safety and well-being.

Recognizing the signs that something may be amiss begins with paying attention to any red flags or discrepancies in job postings, communications, or interviews. If a job opportunity seems too good to be true, promising unrealistically high salaries or extravagant perks, it may be a sign of a scam. Similarly, if the communication from a potential employer is filled with grammatical errors, inconsistent information, or requests for personal and financial details upfront, caution is warranted.

6.2 Providing guidance on conducting thorough research about companies before engaging further

Before proceeding with any job application or further engagement with a potential employer, it is essential to conduct thorough research about the company. This research aims to verify the legitimacy of the organization and ensure that it aligns with your career goals and values.

Start by exploring the company's website and scrutinizing its content for authenticity and professionalism. Look for contact information such as a physical address, email address, and phone number. Cross-reference this information with reputable sources like business directories or professional networking platforms to validate its accuracy.

Additionally, leverage online resources such as company reviews, employee testimonials, and news articles to gather insights into the company's reputation, work culture, and financial stability. This research will enable you to make informed decisions about whether to proceed with the application process or raise concerns about potential scams.

6.3 Offering tips for identifying fake websites, profiles, or contact information used by scammers

Scammers often employ deceptive tactics to create an illusion of legitimacy. They may create fake websites, social media profiles, or contact information mimicking reputable organizations or established companies. Therefore, it is crucial for individuals to develop skills in identifying these fraudulent elements before falling victim to an employment scam.

One effective strategy is to scrutinize website URLs carefully. Look for subtle variations in spelling or domains that differ slightly from legitimate organizations. For example, instead of "companyname.com," scammers may use "company-name.com" or "companyname.org." Additionally, pay attention to the overall design and functionality of the website. Professional companies invest in high-quality design and user-friendly interfaces, whereas scammers may have poorly designed websites with numerous grammatical errors or broken links.

When reviewing social media profiles or contact information provided by potential employers, cross-reference them with verified accounts or contact details from official sources. Look for inconsistencies in profile information, such as conflicting job titles or sparse connections/followers.

Developing these skills will enable individuals to spot fake websites, profiles, or contact information used by scammers and avoid falling into their traps.

6.4 Discussing the importance of consulting others for second opinions on suspicious job offers

It is common for scammers to manipulate individuals through isolation and secrecy. By discouraging victims from seeking second opinions or discussing suspicious job offers with others, scammers increase their chances of success. To counteract this manipulation tactic, it is crucial for individuals to actively seek advice from trusted friends, family members, mentors, or professionals whenever they encounter suspicious job offers.

By sharing details about the job opportunity and any concerns they may have, individuals can benefit from fresh perspectives and objective insights. Others may be able to spot red flags that were overlooked or provide valuable advice based on their own experiences.

Moreover, consider reaching out to professionals in relevant industries who can offer guidance specific to your field of interest. Mentors or career counselors can provide valuable insights on standard practices within your industry and help determine if a job offer aligns with typical expectations.

Engaging with others in discussions about potential employment scams enhances collective awareness and strengthens individuals' ability to protect themselves.

6.5 Sharing personal anecdotes of successful detection of employment scams

To inspire readers and reinforce their ability to recognize employment scams successfully, this chapter will share personal anecdotes of individuals who have detected scams before falling victim.

These stories will depict various scenarios where individuals identified red flags or used their intuition to question a suspicious job offer. By sharing their experiences and detailing how they took appropriate action – such as terminating communication with scammers or reporting the incident – these anecdotes will demonstrate that anyone can develop the skills necessary to protect themselves against employment scams.

The personal narratives will highlight how being vigilant and trusting one's instincts can save individuals from potentially devastating consequences. They will serve as concrete examples of empowerment and encourage readers to continue honing their skills in recognizing employment scams.

By becoming familiar with these real-life stories of successful detection and avoidance of scams, readers will gain confidence in their own abilities to navigate the job market safely.

In Chapter 7: Taking Action When Confronted with the Employment Scam - Steps to Protect Yourself

Chapter 7: Taking Action When Confronted with the Employment Scam

Steps to Protect Yourself

7.1 Outlining Immediate Actions to Take When Suspecting an Employment Scam, Including Ceasing Communication

When you suspect that you may be dealing with an employment scam, it is crucial to take immediate action to protect yourself and minimize potential harm. The first step is to cease all communication with the scammer. Do not respond to their messages, emails, or phone calls. By cutting off contact, you reduce the risk of further manipulation or exploitation.

Furthermore, refrain from providing any additional personal information or financial details. Scammers often use contact information obtained during the application process to target victims with phishing attempts or identity theft. Safeguarding your information is vital in preventing further damage.

7.2 Educating Readers on Preserving Evidence for Potential Legal Action or Reporting Purposes

Preserving evidence is essential if you decide to pursue legal action against scammers or report the incident to relevant authorities. When confronted with an employment scam, make sure to document all communication, including emails, messages, and phone call records. These pieces of evidence can strengthen your case and support any claims you make during legal proceedings.

Additionally, take screenshots or save copies of any job postings, advertisements, or websites related to the scam. These can be valuable evidence to demonstrate fraudulent intent or misrepresentation by the scammers. Remember to date and organize all collected evidence systematically for easy reference in the future.

7.3 Detailing Steps to Safeguard Personal Information from Further Exploitation by Scammers

Once you have cut off communication with the scammers, it is crucial to take steps to safeguard your personal information from further exploitation. Begin by changing passwords for any accounts that may have been compromised during the interaction with the scammer. This includes email accounts, online banking platforms, and social media profiles.

Consider enabling two-factor authentication for added security on your online accounts. This extra layer of protection helps ensure that only authorized individuals can access your accounts, even if they possess your login credentials.

Furthermore, monitor your financial statements and credit reports regularly. Look for any suspicious activity, such as unauthorized transactions or new accounts opened in your name. If you detect any signs of fraudulent activity, notify your bank or credit card company immediately and follow their recommended procedures.

7.4 Discussing Strategies for Recovering Any Financial Losses Caused by the Scam

Recovering from financial losses caused by an employment scam can be a challenging process, but there are strategies that can help mitigate the impact. Start by contacting your local law enforcement agency and reporting the scam. While it may not always result in immediate restitution, it helps create a record of the incident and contributes to building a case against the scammers.

If you provided sensitive financial information during the scam, contact your bank or credit card company right away. Explain the situation and request assistance in monitoring your accounts for any unusual activity. They may be able to reverse fraudulent charges or provide guidance on further steps to protect your finances.

Consider reaching out to nonprofit organizations that specialize in assisting victims of scams. These organizations may offer resources, advice, or even financial support to aid in recovery efforts. Additionally, consult with a reputable financial advisor who can provide guidance on regaining financial stability and creating a plan to rebuild your savings.

7.5 Guiding Readers Through Reporting Procedures to Relevant Authorities and Agencies

Reporting the employment scam to relevant authorities and agencies is crucial not only for personal protection but also for contributing to efforts against scammers. Depending on your location, there may be specific organizations dedicated to handling fraud cases or consumer protection issues.

Start by filing a complaint with your local law enforcement agency, providing them with all relevant evidence and details of the scam. They will guide you through their reporting procedures and assist in investigating the matter further.

Additionally, consider reporting the scam to consumer protection agencies such as the Federal Trade Commission (FTC) or its equivalent in your country. These agencies track fraud trends and use this information to raise awareness and implement countermeasures against scams.

Don't hesitate to report the scam to the platform where you encountered it as well. Online job boards, social media platforms, or other websites want to maintain a safe environment for their users and may take action against scammers based on your complaint.

By reporting the scam, you contribute to collective efforts in combating employment scams and protect others from falling victim to similar schemes.

Chapter 8: Reporting the Employment Scam and Seeking Legal Help

Advancing Justice Against Scammers

8.1 Identifying Appropriate Channels for Reporting an Employment Scam

When confronted with an employment scam, it is crucial to report the incident to the relevant authorities. By reporting these scams, not only can victims help protect themselves and prevent others from falling victim, but they can also contribute to ongoing efforts to combat scammers. This section will provide readers with information on appropriate channels for reporting employment scams, including consumer protection agencies and law enforcement departments.

Readers will be guided through the process of documenting the details of the scam, such as correspondence, screenshots, and any financial transactions involved. It is essential to gather as much evidence as possible to support a potential investigation or legal action against the scammers.

8.2 Discussing Potential Legal Recourse Available for Victims of Employment Scams

Victims of employment scams may find themselves facing significant financial losses or damages due to identity theft or fraudulent activities. In this section, readers will learn about their legal rights and potential legal recourse available to them. The chapter will explore various remedies, such as civil lawsuits or criminal complaints, that victims can pursue against scammers.

It is important to note that legal processes may vary depending on the jurisdiction and the specific circumstances of each case. Readers will be encouraged to seek professional legal advice tailored to their situation to determine the most appropriate course of action.

8.3 Providing Guidance on Gathering Necessary Documentation for Legal Proceedings

To effectively pursue legal action against scammers, victims must compile necessary documentation and evidence. This section will outline the types of evidence required, including any written communications, payment receipts or transaction records, and proof of damages incurred.

Readers will be provided with tips and strategies on organizing and presenting evidence effectively to strengthen their case. Additionally, they will learn about the importance of maintaining careful records throughout the scam incident and recovery process.

8.4 Outlining Resources for Pro Bono Legal Assistance or Affordable Representation

Legal proceedings can be costly and overwhelming for victims of employment scams. However, there are resources available to individuals who may require legal assistance but cannot afford high attorney fees. This section will provide readers with information on pro bono legal services and organizations dedicated to assisting victims of scams.

Readers will learn how to access these resources and understand the eligibility requirements for free or affordable legal representation. It is important for victims to know that they are not alone in seeking justice against scammers and that support is available to them.

8.5 Sharing Success Stories of Individuals Who Have Pursued Legal Action Against Scammers

To inspire hope and showcase the possibility of achieving justice against scammers, this section will share success stories from individuals who have pursued legal action after falling victim to an employment scam. These stories will highlight different outcomes, including monetary restitution, conviction of scammers, and closure for victims.

By sharing these success stories, readers will gain insight into the complexities of pursuing legal action and understand the potential outcomes they can aspire to achieve. These stories serve as a reminder that standing up against scammers can make a difference not just for individual victims but for society as a whole.

Through reporting employment scams and seeking legal help, victims can take an active role in advancing justice against scammers. By following the guidance outlined in this chapter, readers will be empowered with knowledge and resources to navigate the often complex process of seeking justice while holding scammers accountable for their actions.

Chapter 9: Recovering from the Financial and Emotional Impact of the Employment Scam

Rebuilding Your Life

9.1 Addressing the Emotional Toll of Falling Victim to an Employment Scam

Recovering from the aftermath of an employment scam involves not only addressing the financial impact but also acknowledging and healing from the emotional toll it takes. Victims often experience a range of emotional responses, including shock, anger, betrayal, and a sense of violation. It is essential to recognize these feelings as valid and understand that recovery involves both practical steps and emotional healing.

This chapter will delve into the emotional aspects of recovering from an employment scam, providing insights on coping mechanisms and strategies to regain emotional well-being. Understanding that one is not alone in the recovery process can provide solace and hope for victims who may feel isolated.

9.2 Offering Strategies for Regaining Financial Stability after a Loss

One of the immediate challenges victims face after falling for an employment scam is the financial fallout. In some cases, individuals may have lost substantial sums of money or incurred massive debt due to fraudulent activity. Rebuilding one's financial stability can be a daunting task, but there are strategies and resources available to help victims navigate this process.

This chapter will offer practical advice on regaining financial stability after an employment scam, including steps such as contacting financial institutions to report fraudulent activity, working with credit counselors to address any damage to credit scores, and exploring options for debt management or repayment plans. Additionally, it will highlight resources available for seeking legal restitution or compensation, such as victim compensation funds or assistance programs.

9.3 Discussing Options for Credit Repair or Rebuilding Savings Post-Scam

Employment scams can have long-lasting effects on victims' credit scores and savings. It is crucial to provide guidance on repairing damaged credit or rebuilding savings following a scam incident. This chapter will outline steps victims can take to repair their credit, including obtaining free copies of credit reports, disputing fraudulent charges or accounts, and working with credit repair agencies if necessary.

Furthermore, it will explore strategies for rebuilding savings post-scam, such as developing a realistic budget, exploring additional income sources, and seeking financial guidance from trusted professionals or organizations specializing in financial recovery.

9.4 Providing Resources for Accessing Counseling or Support Groups

Recovery from an employment scam involves more than just financial restoration; it also entails addressing emotional trauma and seeking support from others who have had similar experiences. This chapter will provide resources for accessing counseling services or support groups specifically tailored to victims of scams.

By connecting with professionals trained in trauma therapy or joining support groups comprised of individuals who have navigated similar challenges, victims can find solace, validation, and guidance on their journey towards healing.

9.5 Sharing Stories of Resilience and Hope from Individuals Who Have Overcome Similar Experiences

To inspire readers and offer a glimmer of hope during the recovery process, this chapter will share stories of individuals who have triumphed over employment scams and successfully rebuilt their lives. These stories will highlight the strength and resilience demonstrated by survivors and provide insight into effective strategies they employed during their recovery journeys.

By showcasing real-life examples of individuals who have overcome similar challenges, readers will gain inspiration and motivation to persevere through their own recovery processes. These stories will serve as a reminder that recovery is possible and that there is light at the end of the tunnel for those affected by employment scams.

Conclusion:

Recovering from the financial and emotional impact of an employment scam is a multifaceted process that requires both practical steps and emotional healing. By addressing the emotional toll of the scam, offering strategies for regaining financial stability, discussing options for credit repair or rebuilding savings, providing resources for accessing counseling or support groups, and sharing stories of resilience and hope, this chapter aims to guide victims towards a path of recovery.

It is crucial to remember that recovery takes time and that every individual's journey will be unique. By seeking support from professionals, utilizing available resources, and leaning on the strength within themselves, victims can rebuild their lives and emerge stronger than ever before. With perseverance and resilience, it is possible to move forward from the devastating impact of an employment scam and reclaim one's life with renewed hope and optimism.

Chapter 10: Supporting a Friend Who is Falling for the Employment Scam

Helping Others Navigate Scammer Interactions

10.1 Recognizing Signs That a Friend May Be Falling Victim to an Employment Scam

One of the most challenging situations is when we suspect that a friend or loved one may be falling victim to an employment scam. It is crucial to be proactive and attentive to their behavior, as scammers often exploit individuals' trust and manipulate them into making harmful decisions. In this chapter, we will explore the signs that indicate a friend may be falling victim to an employment scam and how we can help them navigate through this difficult situation.

Some common signs that someone may be falling for an employment scam include:

- Expressing sudden excitement about a job opportunity that seems too good to be true.

- Sharing details about unusual or suspicious interview processes.

- Mentioning requests for personal or financial information early in the hiring process.

- Showing concerns about payment methods or receiving excessive advance payments.

- Ignoring or dismissing red flags despite being pointed out by others.

By familiarizing ourselves with these signs, we can better understand when our friends may be at risk and take necessary action.

10.2 Offering Advice on Initiating Conversations About Potential Scams Without Causing Offense or Defensiveness

Approaching a friend who might be falling for an employment scam requires sensitivity and care. It is essential to create a safe space where they feel comfortable discussing their experiences without judgment or defensiveness.

When initiating conversations about potential scams, consider the following advice:

- Choose an appropriate setting where your friend feels comfortable sharing their thoughts and concerns.

- Use open-ended questions to encourage dialogue and allow them to express themselves fully.

- Listen actively and attentively, showing empathy and understanding throughout the conversation.

- Avoid blaming or criticizing them for not recognizing the scam earlier; instead, focus on providing support and guidance.

- Offer resources and information, presenting them as options rather than imposing solutions.

By approaching these conversations with empathy and understanding, you can foster an environment that encourages your friend to share their experiences openly.

10.3 Providing Resources to Educate Friends About Common Red Flags and Prevention Measures

To effectively support our friends in navigating employment scams, it is crucial to provide them with resources that educate them about common red flags and preventive measures. By empowering them with knowledge, they can become more vigilant and less susceptible to scammers' manipulation tactics.

Some helpful resources to share with your friends include:

- Websites and online forums dedicated to scam awareness and prevention.

- Articles or publications by reputable sources that discuss common employment scam tactics.

- Videos or webinars led by experts in cybersecurity or criminal psychology.

- Books that delve deeper into scam prevention strategies.

By sharing these resources, you are equipping your friends with valuable tools that can assist them in making informed decisions during their job search.

10.4 Outlining Methods for Supporting Friends Emotionally During Recovery From a Scam

Recovering from an employment scam can be emotionally challenging for victims. As friends, our role is not only to provide practical advice but also to offer emotional support throughout the recovery process.

Here are some ways you can support your friends emotionally:

- Validate their feelings by acknowledging their vulnerability and empathizing with their experience.

- Encourage them to seek professional help if needed, such as counseling or therapy services.

- Engage in activities that promote self-care and stress relief, such as exercise, meditation, or hobbies.

- Remind them of their strengths and accomplishments outside of the scam incident.

- Maintain regular communication while respecting their need for space or privacy.

Remember, emotional recovery takes time, and everyone heals at their own pace. By being there for your friends consistently, you can help them rebuild their confidence and trust after falling victim to an employment scam.

Chapter 11: Conclusion

A Call to Action

11.1 Summarizing Key Takeaways from Previous Chapters

Throughout the preceding chapters, we have explored the insidious nature of the employment scam and its devastating impact on victims. We have delved into the tactics employed by scammers, analyzed their psychological manipulation techniques, and drawn parallels with other common scams. Additionally, we have discussed the red flags to watch out for and provided strategies to protect oneself from falling victim to an employment scam.

We have also examined the importance of recognizing the signs of a scam, taking immediate action when confronted with one, and seeking legal help and support for recovery. Furthermore, we have explored ways in which individuals can support friends who may be falling prey to employment scams and discussed the role of collective efforts in combating this issue.

11.2 Reinforcing the Importance of Spreading Awareness about Employment Scams

Armed with knowledge and insights gained from this book, readers are now empowered to recognize and combat employment scams. However, this knowledge is not meant to be hoarded but shared with others. Awareness is key in preventing future victims from falling into the clutches of scammers. By spreading knowledge about employment scams, readers can contribute to creating a safer online environment for all.

11.3 Encouraging Readers to Share Knowledge Gained from this Book with Their Communities

It is crucial for readers to take an active role in disseminating the information they have learned throughout this book. By sharing their knowledge with friends, family members, colleagues, and even their wider communities, readers can help others recognize and avoid employment scams. Education is the first line of defense against scammers, and it is through collective efforts that we can make a significant impact in reducing the prevalence of employment scams.

11.4 Issuing a Call to Action for Individuals to Remain Vigilant against Scammers

While this book equips readers with valuable tools and insights, it is essential to remain vigilant in an ever-evolving landscape of scams. Scammers constantly adapt their tactics, making it crucial for individuals to stay informed about emerging threats and new techniques employed by scammers. By staying educated and proactive, readers can stay one step ahead of scammers and protect themselves and those around them.

11.5 Inspiring Hope that Collective Efforts Can Lead to a Safer Online Environment

Fighting against employment scams is not a battle that can be won alone; it requires collective efforts from individuals, communities, businesses, and law enforcement agencies. Through collaboration and a shared commitment to combatting scams, we can create a safer online environment where job seekers can pursue opportunities with confidence.

By raising awareness, holding scammers accountable through reporting mechanisms, supporting victims on their paths to recovery, sharing success stories of triumph over scams, and advocating for ongoing education on cybersecurity and scams, we can work towards eradicating the scourge of employment scams.

Together, let us leverage our collective power and build a future where potential victims are equipped with the knowledge to identify scams before falling prey to deception. It is through our combined efforts that we can make a difference and dismantle the infrastructure that supports employment scams.

Chapter 12: A Message of Hope:

Empowering Individuals Against Scammers - Embracing Resilience

12.1 Highlighting Stories of Individuals Who Have Triumphed Over Employment Scams

In the face of adversity, triumph and resilience are powerful forces that can help individuals overcome the aftermath of an employment scam. This chapter will shine a spotlight on stories of individuals who have successfully navigated through the challenges posed by scams and emerged stronger than ever.

These stories will provide inspiration and serve as examples of how individuals can rebuild their lives after falling victim to an employment scam. They will showcase not only the strength and determination of these individuals but also their ability to learn from their experiences and use them as stepping stones for personal growth.

12.2 Sharing Motivational Messages and Affirmations to Boost Readers' Confidence

Recovering from an employment scam requires a significant amount of emotional strength and resilience. In this section, readers will find motivational messages and affirmations specifically crafted to uplift their spirits and help them regain confidence in themselves.

By internalizing positive affirmations such as "I am resilient," "I am capable of overcoming challenges," and "I am worthy of success," readers can begin to shift their mindset from one of victimhood to one of empowerment. These messages will serve as daily reminders that they have the power to overcome adversity and build a better future for themselves.

12.3 Offering Practical Advice on Building Positive Online Experiences

After encountering an employment scam, individuals may feel hesitant or fearful when engaging with online platforms. This section will provide practical advice on how to navigate the online landscape safely while minimizing the risk of falling victim to scams.

Readers will learn about essential cybersecurity practices, such as utilizing strong, unique passwords, enabling two-factor authentication, and being cautious when sharing personal information online. Additionally, they will gain insights into recognizing secure websites, verifying the legitimacy of online job postings, and conducting thorough research on potential employers before engaging further.

12.4 Advocating for Continued Education on Cybersecurity and Scams

To combat the ever-evolving tactics used by scammers, ongoing education is crucial. This section will emphasize the importance of continuously educating oneself about cybersecurity best practices and staying informed about the latest scams.

Readers will be provided with resources such as online courses, webinars, and workshops that focus on cybersecurity awareness. By actively seeking out opportunities for learning and staying up-to-date with emerging scams, readers can remain one step ahead of scammers and protect themselves more effectively.

12.5 Conveying a Message That Everyone Has the Power to Protect Themselves from Scammers

In conclusion, this chapter will reinforce the overarching message that everyone possesses the inherent power to protect themselves from scammers. By adhering to preventative measures, staying vigilant, and relying on knowledge gained from this book, readers can significantly reduce their susceptibility to employment scams.

Readers will be reminded that they do not need to be victims; they have the ability to make informed choices, exercise caution when interacting online, and empower themselves against scammers. The chapter will end with a call to action, encouraging readers to embrace their inner resilience and commit to taking proactive steps in securing their futures.

Throughout this book, we have explored the anatomy of the employment scam from various angles – understanding its scope and impact, unraveling tactics employed by scammers, delving into psychological manipulation techniques, identifying similarities with other common scams, recognizing warning signs, reporting scams, seeking legal help, recovering from financial and emotional impacts, supporting friends who may be falling victim, and embracing resilience.

Armed with knowledge and empowered by personal anecdotes and motivational messages, readers are now equipped to navigate the digital landscape with greater confidence. Remember: You have the power to protect yourself. Together, let us forge a path towards a safer online environment for all.

Chapter 13: Additional Resources for Protection Against Employment Scams

Expanding Knowledge and Support Network

13.1 Listing Trusted Websites, Books, and Articles Related to Scam Prevention

To further enhance readers' understanding of employment scams and provide additional resources for protection, this chapter will provide a comprehensive list of trusted websites, books, and articles that delve deeper into the subject matter. These resources have been carefully selected based on their credibility, expertise, and relevance to scam prevention.

Readers can visit these websites to access valuable information, guides, and tools to protect themselves against employment scams. These resources may offer insights on identifying red flags, reporting scams, seeking legal assistance, recovering from financial loss, and rebuilding after falling victim to a scam.

13.2 Recommending Online Forums or Support Groups for Victims or Potential Victims

In addition to educational resources, online forums and support groups play a crucial role in connecting victims or potential victims of employment scams. These platforms provide a safe space for individuals to share their experiences, seek advice, and find emotional support from others who have gone through similar situations.

This chapter will recommend reputable online forums or support groups where readers can engage with the community, share stories, and gain insights into navigating the aftermath of an employment scam. The focus will be on platforms that prioritize anonymity, privacy, and moderation to ensure a supportive and constructive environment.

13.3 Providing Contact Information for Consumer Protection Organizations

When confronted with an employment scam or seeking guidance on scam prevention, contacting consumer protection organizations can be immensely helpful. These organizations specialize in providing assistance to individuals who have fallen victim to scams or are looking for ways to protect themselves from potential fraud.

This chapter will provide readers with contact information for reputable consumer protection organizations that handle employment scams specifically. These organizations may offer dedicated hotlines, online complaint forms, or email addresses where victims can report scams and seek assistance in navigating the legal and recovery processes.

13.4 Suggesting Online Courses or Workshops on Cybersecurity Awareness

As technology continues to evolve rapidly, it is imperative to stay informed about cybersecurity best practices and online safety measures. This chapter will suggest online courses or workshops focused on cybersecurity awareness to equip readers with essential knowledge and skills to navigate the digital landscape securely.

These courses may cover topics such as identifying online threats, securing personal information online, recognizing phishing attempts, and protecting against identity theft. By participating in these educational programs, readers can enhance their understanding of cybersecurity risks related to employment scams and strengthen their overall online safety practices.

13.5 Including Hotline Numbers for Immediate Assistance in Reporting Scams

When individuals encounter an employment scam or suspect fraudulent activity, immediate reporting is crucial. This chapter will include hotline numbers that readers can call for immediate assistance in reporting scams to relevant authorities or agencies. These hotlines may be specific to employment scams or fall under the jurisdiction of consumer protection agencies or law enforcement bodies responsible for investigating fraudulent activities.

Providing readily accessible hotline numbers ensures that readers have a quick means of reporting scams without delay. The prompt reporting of scams enhances the chances of preventing further harm and facilitates swift action against scammers.

By expanding readers' knowledge and support network through trusted resources and contact information, this chapter aims to provide comprehensive assistance to individuals seeking protection against employment scams. Empowering readers with additional tools and avenues for support strengthens their ability to detect, prevent, and recover from potential scam incidents effectively.

NOTE: All recommended websites, books, articles, forums/support groups, consumer protection organizations, online courses/workshops, and hotline numbers should undergo thorough vetting to ensure their legitimacy and trustworthiness before including them in this chapter.

Chapter 14: Author's Closing Thoughts and Acknowledgments

Expressing Gratitude and Final Reflections

14.1 Reflecting on Personal Experiences with Employment Scams

As I reach the end of this informative journey on the anatomy of the employment scam, I cannot help but reflect on my own personal experiences with this pervasive issue. Like many others, I too have encountered various forms of scams throughout my life, including those targeting employment seekers. These encounters have served as a catalyst for my desire to raise awareness and provide individuals with the necessary tools to protect themselves from such deceitful schemes.

By delving deep into the world of employment scams, it became evident that scammers prey on vulnerability, hope, and the innate desire for financial stability. The stories shared by victims have touched me deeply and reinforced the importance of shedding light on this issue. It is my hope that through this book, readers are inspired to remain vigilant, educated, and proactive in their interactions online.

14.2 Expressing Gratitude Towards Individuals who Supported During the Book-Writing Process

I would like to express my sincere gratitude to all those who supported and contributed to the creation of this book. First and foremost, I am thankful to the individuals who shared their personal experiences with employment scams. Your willingness to open up and recount your stories has been crucial in raising awareness and fostering empathy among our readers.

I extend my appreciation to all the experts in cybersecurity, criminology, psychology, and scam prevention who provided valuable insights and expertise throughout this writing process. Your knowledge helped shape the content in a way that is both educational and engaging.

A special thanks goes out to my family and friends for their unwavering support and encouragement. Your belief in me fueled my determination to complete this project.

Finally, I want to express my deepest appreciation to the readers of this book. Thank you for investing your time and trust in this endeavor. It is my greatest hope that you will find the information within these pages valuable and empowering.

14.3 Offering Final Words of Encouragement, Emphasizing Collective Efforts Against Scams

As we come to a close, I want to leave you with a final message of encouragement. The fight against employment scams requires collective efforts from individuals, communities, organizations, and law enforcement agencies. By sharing the knowledge gained from this book with others in your community, you can contribute to creating a safer online environment for everyone.

Remember that education is key in defending ourselves against scams' ever-evolving tactics. Stay informed about emerging trends, technological advancements, and safeguarding measures. Together, we can fortify our defenses and make it increasingly difficult for scammers to succeed in their deceitful endeavors.

14.4 Encouraging Readers to Stay Vigilant, Informed, and Proactive

As you conclude this book, I urge you to stay vigilant in your interactions online. Always be cautious when providing personal information or engaging in financial transactions. Trust your instincts and listen to that inner voice when something feels off during your job search or recruitment process.

Remain informed about potential red flags and warning signs specific to employment scams while continually educating yourself on other types of scams as well. The more knowledgeable you are, the better equipped you will be to identify and avoid potential dangers.

Above all, remain proactive in creating a safer digital landscape. Report any suspicious activity or encounters with scammers promptly. Advocate for stronger consumer protection laws and cybersecurity measures within your communities. Your actions can make a significant difference in preventing others from falling victim to employment scams.

14.5 Thanking Readers for Their Commitment to Combatting Common Scams

In closing, I want to express my utmost gratitude once again for embarking on this educational journey with me. Your commitment to combatting common scams deserves recognition. By equipping yourself with knowledge and sharing it with others, you are playing an instrumental role in safeguarding individuals from falling prey to employment scams.

Together, let us continue spreading awareness, supporting one another through acts of kindness, and embracing resilience in combating scams of all kinds. With each step forward, we move closer toward creating a digital world where trust prevails over deceit.

Thank you for your dedication, support, and ongoing commitment to empowering individuals against scammers. Stay vigilant, stay informed, and always trust your instincts.

Wishing you a safe and prosperous future,

Hon. Thomas Mitchell, DD, PhD

Lord of Kerry, Republic of Ireland

AUTHOR

Hon. Thomas Mitchell, DD, PhD

Lord of Kerry, Republic of Ireland

Knight, Order of Minerva